THE Corset AND THE Loom

A Tapestry of Poetry and Prose

By

BRANDY LANE

WHERE BEAUTIFUL INKS LLC

Fort Wayne, Indiana

Published in the United States of America by
Where Beautiful Inks LLC
Fort Wayne, Indiana

ISBN: 978-1-970359-01-5
Library of Congress Control Number: 2025923699

Cover made with AI on Canva Pro under Where Beautiful Inks LLC
All pictures throughout this book are available through Canva and Canva Pro.

Dedication

"For those who have loved, unraveled, and dared to weave again."

And, as always, for my Dragon.
-Brandy

Prologue

This is where the unraveling began—in silence, in shadow, and in the soft hum of thread remembering its purpose.

Trudging through the doldrums and the decayed remnants of dreams no longer mine, I followed the mellifluous echoes that wound through the silent halls. Shadows stretched long across the walls, curling like smoke around faded portraits and splintered banisters, and each step drew me closer to a music that was both haunting and sweet.

The sounds grew warmer, richer, a harmony that seemed almost alive, tugging at a place deep within my chest. I reached the door at last, hand trembling with a mix of trepidation and longing, and pushed it open.

Before me, a room bloomed in the soft glow of candlelight, filled with jovial spirits whose laughter danced like silver threads through the air. They moved as though tethered by invisible cords of delight, sharing glances, whispered jokes, and the tender intimacy of presence. For a moment, I felt like an intruder, yet the warmth pressed gently against my chest, drawing me in.

I lingered at the threshold, mesmerized, feeling both the ache of what was absent in my own life and the bittersweet beauty of connection I could only watch from afar. The echoes of music and mirth wrapped around me, a haunting lullaby of love, loss, and the ghost of hope still flickering in quiet corners.

And as I finally stepped inside, the door closed softly behind me, leaving only the faintest whisper of the world I had left behind, and the possibility that perhaps even in shadowed halls, joy could bloom again.

Brandy Lane

Table of Contents

The Corset and the Loom

The Thread

Tangled Up in You

In the thread, we remember.

Threads of You
PART I

I was swept into your storm,
a dust-bun in cathedral light,
tossed between shadow and memory,
until the floor I knew vanished beneath me.

You stirred me with a glance,
a whisper,
and I twirled in currents unnamed,
lost between the chaos of myself,
and the brilliance—you passed like a comet.

Where is the joy I brought to you?
Did you hide it behind shuttered arches,
or scatter it into corners
where sunlight dares not enter?

The laughter we shared, once bright,
now trembles only in hollow halls,
echoing faintly through cold stone.
I speak to you through hands that are stilled,
though my body cannot follow
where my heart lingers.

Every word is a fragile echo of touch,
a brush of hair, a fleeting wish,
a heart that loves beyond the compass of language,
anchored still in what once was.

We were threads spun of shadow and silk,
woven in longing's deliberate loom.
Every caress drew us taut,
every silence stitched a hidden scar.

Now you have unbraided us,
leaving me kinked, frayed,
a soft tension that remembers
the shape of your hands
and the reverberations of our embrace.

You glide through polished light,
while I linger on serrated edges,
yet even here, in this dim spire of memory,
the wind murmurs your name.

I remember the waltz,
the dizzying turn,
how we sparkled—entwined,
how, even in shadows, we moved as one.

Threads Reclaimed

PART 2

The morning spills across the floor,
soft light brushing the edges of memory.
I rise from shadow, untangled,
catching threads that once frayed in your storm.

Your laughter lingers still,
a gentle echo among the dust motes.
I reach for it, not to hold,
but to let it warm the space I inhabit.

Hands may not follow,
yet the heart moves freely,
and in its quiet orbit
your presence bends around me,
softening, steadying,
as though it had never left.

We are threads, still spun together,
but now the loom is wider,
and the light falls differently—
illuminating not just what was lost,
but what may be found again.

Even in absence, there is pulse,
a cadence that teaches the eyes to see
and the body to remember
the gentle art of rising,
of stepping into wind
and letting it carry you lightly,
without fear of fray.

Your name passes through me,
not as longing or ache,
but as a warmth that lingers,
a gift of quiet constancy.
And though the storm has passed,
I walk forward, still tethered,
still believing
in the delicate dance
that waits when light allows.

Waltz of Dust and Light

PART 3

I spun—a glimmer of gold
skipping over sunbeams like stepping stones—
tripping, laughing,
tossed into the sky by invisible hands.

The air smells like candied pecans, and rain,
and you—
you are a laugh caught in the swirl,
a shadow that bends with the light,
a music only I can hear.

The cats twirl with me,
their fur a confetti gown,
and I am dizzy,
yet flying in ways the floor cannot know.
No gravity, no sorrow, only the flit of us—
a carousel of warmth and motion.

Even your absence hums with color,
like ribbons caught in a draft,
reminding me that the waltz continues
even when we are apart.

I reach, I tumble, I soar,
and the wind answers with a wink,
holding the memory of your hands
as if it knew the dance by heart.

Here, there is no fracture,
no kinked threads,
only motion,
and the gleam of infinite possibility
looping through the corners of the day.

I am alive,
and so is what you gave me—
an unbroken melody,
a playful spark
that flutters in the light
even when you are gone.

The Tapestry

It began with a single thread—
a loose shimmer at the corner of us.
You noticed first, fingers brushing it back
like a stray lock of hair.
I pretended not to see.

The tapestry was the color of all the blues—
indigo for the nights we survived,
cobalt for laughter in the rain,
and cerulean—soft as your eyes
when you looked at me and didn't flinch.

Each morning, I tried to mend it.
A stitch here, a knot there—
hope disguised as handiwork.
But the weave grew thinner,
the threads brittle with time and silence.

Soon the patterns began to fade—
the constellations we once traced,
the warmth of our shared horizon.

The loom creaked under the strain,
and still I pulled, I tied, I prayed.

When it finally came apart,
I gathered what remained—
the tangled threads, the ghost of the design—
and pressed them to my heart
as if holding fast could make them whole.

Even now, when light hits just right,
I swear I see it again—
the shimmer, the blue, the promise.
And though my fingers bleed from trying,
I cannot stop from weaving you back.

.

From What was Left of Dreaming

The night was long—
its echoes stitched with thunder,
its silence weighted by ghosts of rain.
But morning came anyway,
unfolding itself in tender gold.

I rose from what was left of dreaming,
bare feet brushing the threads I'd woven—
those blues and silvers, the sigh of old love—
and found, between them, something bright.

It was not what I had planned to make,
nor what the past had promised.
But there it was—
soft as breath, strong as mercy—
a new beginning, glimmering pale as dawn.

I took it up, hands steady this time,
and wove not for memory, but for life.
The threads no longer mourned—they sang,
their hum an offering to what endures:

that love, even when it frays,
leaves color in the hands that held it;
that loss, when met with grace,
can bloom into design.

Now the cloth shimmers—
not perfect, but alive—
each thread catching light
like forgiveness come home.

And when the wind moves through it,
I do not think of endings.
Only of how beautifully
the morning holds what remains.

Reweaving My Love

When it was gone, the loom sat silent—
the air thick with the ghost of thread.
For weeks, I couldn't bear to touch it,
the spindles whispering of all I'd lost.

But one morning, when the light slanted soft,
I found a single strand left behind—
a pale blue filament, thin as forgiveness,
still warm from where your hand had been.

I held it up to the window.
It caught the sun and shimmered,
and something in me—small and trembling—
remembered how to breathe again.

I didn't try to rebuild what was.
Some beauty can't be repeated,
nor should it be.
Instead, I began anew—slowly, quietly—
weaving from what remained.

Now the cloth grows strange and lovely,
woven through with all our ghosts.
Azure for what I miss,
silver for what endured,
and white—for what I've learned to let go.

It does not look like love once did,
but it holds the same pulse,
the same devotion to light.
When the breeze moves through it,
it hums your name—
soft, but whole.

Echoes in the Hall

I trudge through the doldrums,
through the decayed remnants of dreams no longer mine.
The mellifluous echoes thread through the halls,
winding, tugging, alive.

Shadows stretch long across walls,
curling like smoke around faded portraits,
splintered banisters, broken thresholds.
Each step draws me closer,
a pull in the chest I cannot name.

At the door, I pause.
My hand hovers, trembling,
then pushes through the warmth of candlelight.

Inside, a room blooms.
Spirits move with quiet joy,
laughter and whispers curling through the air
like silver threads.
They are tethered together,
and I am separate,
but the warmth presses gently against me,
pulling me into the space I almost fear to claim.

I linger,
the ache of absence pressing soft against my ribs,
the bittersweet taste of connection
I can only watch, only feel.
The music hums,
the mirth wraps me in a delicate veil,
haunting, tender, alive.

And I step inside.
The door closes softly behind me.
A single pulse lingers,
a presence that feels like hope,
and even here, in shadowed halls,
something blooms again.

Split Ends

We were woven once—
a single, shining strand,
our thoughts like silk threads
pulled from the same cocoon.

Now I find myself unraveling,
each memory a filament snapping,
each dream a tangle of what was.

You've gone smooth again,
polished, unbothered—
while I remain here,
frayed and uneven,
still curling toward your warmth
like hair that won't stop remembering
the braid it once belonged to.

The Corset

The Structure of Love

In the corset, we are shaped.

The Corset Binds

It is not fury that fastens breath to bone,
but gentle art that bids the shape be known.
The silken cord, the measured, tender bind—
it frames the form, yet tames the wayward mind.

So love constrains, though softly, not unkind,
a ribbon wound through heart and thought entwined.
It shapes the soul as boning shapes the waist,
in beauty's name, though breath must be displaced.

And poetry—its sister craft and twin—
holds passion still, that it might dwell within.
Each line a stay, each rhyme a gilded seam,
that binds the body of a fleeting dream.

Yet seams will sigh, and stays at last will part—
and loose the trembling fabric of the heart.
Then, gasping free, we bless what held us fast,
for what is love, if not the shape it casts?

Structured and Refined

Torment is not what tightens heart to frame—
but devotion measured in inches,
breath pulled taut beneath brocade and silk.
Every ribbon whispers restraint,
and every knot is a vow not to unravel.

Love, too, demands its shaping—
it cinches, molds, defines the heart's wild form.
We call it passion, but it is also discipline:
the staying, the binding, the deliberate pull
of words stitched tight around longing.

Poetry is no different—
a body bound by meter, a soul pressed into rhyme,
yet within its frame, the pulse grows fierce.
The tighter the lines, the truer the ache—
beauty straining against its own perfection.

And when the stays at last give way,
when the seams sigh open,
we breathe again—bruised, remade,
and whisper to the loosened laces:
you held me, and I became.

The Bones, Not the Corset

We laid the rules
    like boards in careful rows,
counted tokens,
    measured every turn—
each move a vow,
    each silence something owed,
each flame we lit
    a lesson left to burn.

But love—
    love slipped between the tiles and dice,
laughed at order,
    mocked the score;
and when we tried to cage it—twice—
    it broke the frame,
        then asked for more.

We thought we'd mastered every game,
    the bones of play,
        the points hard-won—
but love—it fits the bones the same,
    just not the rigid corset of one.

It breathes between
    the rule and chance,
the house we build,
    the stars we shun—
and every loss becomes romance
    when hearts declare,
        the game's begun.

And when the pieces fade to dust,
    love waits—uncharted, keeping trust.

So play again—
    no need to win,
for love resets
    where rules grow thin.

Fits the Bones

It fits the bones, the quiet frame beneath,
yet chafes against the rules, the structured sheath.
Each card, each die, each carefully laid tile
seeks order, measure, cadence all the while.

But love arrives, a breath of untamed air,
it bends the edges of the strictest snare.
A pawn steps boldly where the board forbade,
and hearts, like rivers, weave their own cascade.

The rules may whisper, precise, austere, confined,
yet hands entwined unbind what was designed.
What once seemed rigid, narrow, sharply spun
now folds to warmth—the game is overrun.

Here, love is not a law, but gentle art,
it loosens what was pressed against the heart.
No board can bind what dances in the chest,
no rule can claim the freedom of our rest.

Each unlatched loop, each knot that slips apart,
is mirrored in the loosening of the heart.
And in that quiet, tender, whispered pause,
the game dissolves beneath the lover's laws.

Unlacing the Corset

Each stitch, each thread, each carefully placed pin
seeks order, measure, cadence, to still breathe within.

Fingers trace the seams, the fastened rows,
a delicate surrender no one knows.
Buttons undone, laces fall away,
the structure softens, yielding to the sway.

The night was laced in whispered thread,
a rule too tight around the heart;
each breath we drew was measured,
fed to form, to pattern, to the art.

But you—
you touched the stay, unpinned the seam,
and every binding line grew kind.
The world exhaled—a loosened dream,
where breath and body intertwined.

No scandal here,
just mercy's hand—
the bones released, the silk undone.
The rules that once could make us stand
now teach us how to fall as one.

The stars looked down and did not chide,
for even order must confess—
there's beauty in the things untied,
and grace within the loosened dress.

The Shape of Love

It is not cruelty that laces bone to bone,
but gentle art that bids the shape be known.
The silken cord draws close—
not to suffocate,
but to remind the body
how beauty requires restraint.

So love constrains, though softly, not unkind.
It shapes the soul the way boning shapes the waist—
in beauty's name, though breath must sometimes falter.

And poetry—its sister craft—
does much the same.
Each line a stay, each rhyme a careful seam,
binding the trembling fabric of a dream.

But seams do sigh, and stays grow weary.
The body, the poem, the heart—
all ache to be unfastened.

And when at last the ties give way,
we bless what once held us fast.
For what is love,
if not the shape it leaves behind?

Different Rules for Cruelty

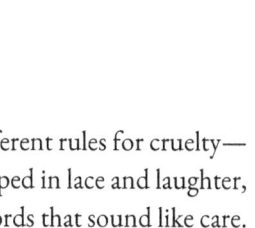

There are different rules for cruelty—
those wrapped in lace and laughter,
those dressed in words that sound like care.
It's the quiet ones that wound the deepest,
the hands that linger too long on the laces
before they pull them tighter.

There is cruelty in beauty—
in the way the corset loves and imprisons,
the way poetry can gild the pain
until it gleams like reverence.
It whispers hold still, don't breathe, be perfect.
And we obey, because it feels like love.

There are cruelties without villains—
the well-meaning seams,
the careful stitches that shape what we are not.
We smile through the ache,
call the bruises devotion,
and name the suffocation art.

When it's over,
we look upon the ruin—
the loosened stays, the trembling ribs—
and cannot tell if what broke
was the binding or the heart.

At the Seams

There is a hush between the strands,
a pause where meaning slips away.
The needle waits, the pattern fades,
and daylight folds to muted gray.

I trace the threads that used to bind,
their shimmer dulled, their promise thin.
What once was whole now comes apart—
unraveling beneath my skin.

The Unbinding

The hour is late, and the mirror sighs.
Threads loosen, slow as confession,
and silk remembers every tremor of touch.

One ribbon slips free—then another—
like the shedding of promises once spoken in fire.
The fabric falls in quiet folds,
a surrender without shame.

Beneath the loosened seams,
the skin breathes again—raw, forgiven.
What once was form now finds its truth in formlessness.
The ribs expand, the heart recalls its music,
and every sigh becomes a psalm of freedom.

No bitterness remains.
Only the ghost of beauty—
and the tender ache
of having been so perfectly held.

The Unlearning of Discipline

The ties fall away.
The air remembers its shape.
In stillness, the thread stirs—
ready to be born again.

Empty hands tremble once,
then reach for color.
What was restraint,
becomes design.

Breath gathers,
thread awakens.
Between what was held
and what is made—
the loom hums softly.

The hands unlearn,
then begin.

The Loom

Woven in the Heart

In the loom, we are remade.

Lapis Threads

You wore your faith around your neck—
a cross of gilt and heavy sorrow,
its lapis heart a frozen speck
of sky, once bright with borrowed morrow.

I held it once and felt the chill,
the metal's weight, the hollow sound—
and knew that faith, when held too still,
can turn to stone beneath the ground.

So I began to weave instead,
to spin my prayers in colored thread.
Crimson for love, and gold for grace,
and blue for all I could not face.

Your lapis gleams within the seam,
a shard of heaven in my cloth.
I stitch belief into a dream,
and find the life your sermon lost.

For what you wore as solemn art,
I've spun anew within my heart.

To Begin Again

Her fingers move without thought now,
guided by something older than knowing.
Each movement is both prayer and pulse,
each pattern an echo of what once hurt,
now softened into silk.

She threads the gold through shadow's edge,
humming a tune that only cloth remembers.
No lesson. No doctrine.
Only this quiet forgiveness that grows
between the warp and weft.

Her hands bear colors of all of her toil.
They carry traces of everything she's touched—
the dye of memory, the stain of love,
the faint shimmer of dreams that would not fade.

She has learned
that grace was never in perfection—
but in the patience
to begin again.

Beauty Bloomed

I dip my hands in lapis dye,
staining them with what has been.
Threads of gold and ash entwine,
each a promise, each a sin.

The shuttle hums, the spindle spins,
a heartbeat caught between the twine.
Love begins in whisper-thin
fibers that remember mine.

I weave your voice through every strand,
your laughter in the warp and weft—
a pattern only I can stand
to finish now that you have left.

Each knot remembers where we kissed,
each thread still trembles at your name;
the loom sighs softly, *you exist*,
in color, form, and mortal frame.

And when I'm gone, this cloth will tell
how beauty bloomed and broke the spell.

Between the Making and the Meaning

The loom rests,
threads gleaming with breath.
Between the making
and the meaning—
the heart listens.

What was made in longing
now shimmers with grace.
The hands grow still—
the soul takes up the work.

In the hush that follows creation,
the air hums with what remains—
not sorrow,
not joy,
but the quiet ache
of something complete.

The threads fall silent.
The prayer begins.

The Weaver's Benediction

The weaver hums beneath her breath,
a hymn to love, defying death.
Her shuttle moves—swift, soft, unseen—
through warp of gold and weft of green.

She threads the dusk, she knots the dawn,
she binds what breaks, she mends what's gone.
Each strand remembers where it's been,
each twist conceals the ache within.

She spins the sorrow, spins it bright,
until it gleams with borrowed light.
No tear is lost, no hope misplaced—
the cloth remembers every face.

Her fingers whisper, slow, divine,
"This thread was his, that one was mine."
The pattern shifts, the colors blend—
no start to love, and so—no end.

When twilight falls, the loom is still,
the moonlight drapes her windowsill.
The weaver smiles, her task complete,
and lays her heart beside her seat.

For love is not a thing unspun—
it lives in all the work she's done.
Each thread, each tear, each vow she keeps—
the loom still hums while the weaver sleeps.

The Weaver's Haunting

The loom remembers every cry,
each whispered vow, each long goodbye.
The shuttle stirs through ghostly thread,
the weaver speaks among the dead.

Her fingers ache, her knuckles bleed,
she weaves the living into need.
Each strand a pulse once warm, once near—
now wound in grief, now tied with fear.

The pattern shivers, shifts, decays,
unraveling nights, repeating days.
She hums the names she cannot say,
the ones the light has swept away.

The tapestry begins to moan,
a thousand sighs within its tone.
The cloth turns pale, the edges fray—
still, she cannot look away.

For love, she knows, is never done,
a war half-lost, a race not run.
She weaves and weeps, her heart the cost—
to hold the faces she has lost.

And when the candle burns to gloom,
its wax a shroud across the room,
she lays her cheek against the frame—
and whispers once more your name.

The Weaver's Dream

She dreamed the threads would sing again,
not dirges bound to loss or pain,
but gentle hymns that hummed of spring—
of what the heart remembers, still wanting to bring.

The loom lay silent through the years,
its frame still damp with ghostly tears.
Yet when she touched its oaken side,
a shimmer woke—and time complied.

The strands once gray grew gold anew,
as morning spilled its tender hue;
and every knot that sorrow tied,
unraveled softly, dignified.

She wove the dark, she wove the light,
the laughter brief, the endless night.
Each filament—a soul reborn,
a petal saved from grief's torn thorn.

Her fingers glowed, the warp took flame,
the world renewed, yet still the same.
The pattern bloomed from ash and seam—
and she awoke within her dream.

Now every cloth she weaves will hold
both mourning's ash and morning's gold;
for love endures, though threads may fade—
a tapestry of hearts remade.

The Threadkeeper

The weaver sleeps, her work complete,
yet still the loom begins to beat.
No mortal hands now pull the thread—
the cloth remembers what she said.

Each whispered vow, each lover's sigh,
each teardrop caught before goodbye,
are woven deep in warp and weft,
of all she gave, and all that's left.

The colors shift with morning's gleam,
alive, as though the threads could dream.
They hum with songs the soul once knew,
of everything she loved—and you.

And when the moonlight fades to gray,
and all her tools are locked away,
the tapestry begins to glow,
for love still weaves, though hands let go.

The Weaver's Hands

The weaver's hands are never clean—
they're stained of dye from what's been done,
a trace of sorrow, blue and keen,
the scarlet threads of love begun.

They move like prayer, they move like fire,
tugging beauty from the ache,
each motion born of slow desire,
each pattern proof that hearts can make.

She stitches opal through silhouette's seam,
she sings of faith she's come to know;
no sermon now, no gilded dream,
just cloth that breathes where hands let go.

For in her palms, the past unspools—
and grace is learned outside of rules.

The Thread Between Us

Once I sat beside the loomlight, weaving love into the gloomlight,
listening to the shuttle's whisper where your shadow used to be.
Every strand recalled your laughter, every knot the silence after,
tangled hope and holy rafter—woven ghosts in memory.
"Still he lingers," hummed the spindle—soft, uncertain, full of plea—
"Bound by thread between the we."

All the threads were pale and sighing, some for living, some for dying,
each a vein of bright defiance through the fabric's quiet plea.
I could feel the night's confession, stitched through loss and old possession,
as if sorrow made profession to the craft that set it free.
"Still he lingers," sang the pattern, deep as root and dark as sea—
"Bound by thread between the we."

Then the moon rose, faintly gleaming through the warp's half-waking dreaming,
casting ghosts of gold and silver on the tapestry I'd spun.
And I knew your hands were guiding, though the years had left them hiding,
for the loom itself was chiding, whispering what love had done:
"Still he lingers," breathed the fabric, "heart to heart and endlessly—
Ever bound between the we."

Now I weave through dusk and sorrow, stealing joy from each tomorrow,
trading grief for fleeting color that the dawn might never see.
Every thread a small forgiving, proof that life is still worth living,
even loss, forever giving—its own woven elegy.
"Still he lingers," sighs the silence, "not in death, but tapestry—
Ever bound between the we."

Your Laughter Hums

Crimson is the color I chose,
staining cloth with what's to be.
Silver threads and twilight sighs—
become the dreams you've left with me.

I weave between the threads and sing,
the loom keeps time beneath my palms.
Each filament, a vow it brings,
each knot, a prayer that soothes and calms.

Your laughter hums through every strand,
your warmth still glows within the seam.
We spin a world by our own hand—
a woven hope, a living dream.

And if the fabric ever fray,
our threads will meet in light someday.

Loomsong

The loom hums softly in the fading light,
its rhythm steady as a heartbeat's vow.
Threads gleam like veins beneath her touch,
each strand remembering—then and now.

She weaves in whispers, laughter, rain,
a lock of hair, a sigh, a prayer.
Colors rise like dawn again,
and love takes shape from patient air.

The cloth begins to breathe, to sing,
to tell what only time can know—
that every loss leaves shining string,
and every ending learns to glow.

She leans back, weary, almost new,
her heart still echoing the tune.
The loom falls silent—yet still true,
it hums the song beneath the moon.

Brandy Lane

About the Author
& Where Beautiful Inks LLC

Brandy Lane is a poet, singer, and publisher whose artistry bridges the deeply personal and the universal. She is the author of Where Beautiful Loves I & II, The Briny Sea of Poetry, Unrequited, and Talking to the Moon, as well as the anthologies Winter and Love is Pain I, with Love is Pain II forthcoming. Her poetry, celebrated for its lyrical honesty and evocative imagery, has appeared in more than forty anthologies and literary magazines worldwide.

As the founder of Where Beautiful Inks LLC, Brandy is committed to amplifying diverse voices in contemporary poetry. She has published the solo collections of poets DMTakeshi and Anila Bukhari, and served as publishing consultant for Diane Gollub and Angela Psalm. In addition, she has worked as an editor for Reena Doss, guiding writers through the creative and technical process of bringing their words into the world.

Balancing her roles as creator and curator, Brandy continues to shape today's literary landscape—offering readers not only her own moving verse but also the voices of others whose work might otherwise go unheard.

Where Beautiful Inks is a publishing imprint based in the United States of America. Services include consulting, publishing advisor, formatting, editing, cover design, publishing, mini web design, poetry writing, illustrations (digital collage and hand-drawn), and photography with minor editing.

If you would like more information, please feel free to contact her at the links below (her social media is on the site).

https://wherebeautifullives.my.canva.site/poetryandpublishing